KATE RITCHIE
Everyday Play

For Rebekah, Stuart and Susan and for the kids we were.

PUFFIN BOOKS

UK | USA | Canada | Ireland | Australia
India | New Zealand | South Africa | China

Penguin Random House Australia is part of the Penguin Random House group of companies whose addresses can be found at global.penguinrandomhouse.com.

First published by Puffin Books, an imprint of Penguin Random House Australia Pty Ltd, in 2022

Text copyright © Kate Ritchie 2022
Photographs copyright © Damian Bennett 2022

The moral right of the author has been asserted.

All rights reserved. No part of this publication may be reproduced, published, performed in public or communicated to the public in any form or by any means without prior written permission from Penguin Random House Australia Pty Ltd or its authorised licensees.

Every effort has been made to contact and acknowledge copyright holders for permission to reproduce material contained in this book. Any copyright holders who have been inadvertently omitted should contact the publisher and omissions will be rectified in subsequent editions.

Illustrations, cover and text design by Rebecca King © Penguin Random House Australia Pty Ltd
Photography by Damian Bennett unless noted below
Photographs taken by Damian Bennett at Greyleigh Kiama
Additional internal photographs supplied by the author except:
page 12: girls playing with paper boats – A3pfamily/Shutterstock.com
page 18: pizza – Africa Studio/Shutterstock.com
page 59: girl with doll – Travelpixs/Shutterstock.com
page 70: hummingbird cake – Hinzefoto/Shutterstock.com
page 98: girl writing in journal – Anurak Pongpatimet/Shutterstock.com
page 102: girl sitting in grass – Amelia Fox/Shutterstock.com
page 115: children with magnifying glass – Jacob Lund/Shutterstock.com
page 135: boys camping – Vasilyev Alexandr/Shutterstock.com
pages 142–43: girls singing – Syda Productions/Shutterstock.com
page 160: rocky road – Kolpakova Svetlana/Shutterstock.com
Street art on page 50 by Jamie Preisz, used with permission
Illustrations created by Rebecca King along with some wonderful contributions from Mae, as well as from Isla, Peter, Leroy, Mia and Polly

Printed and bound in China

 A catalogue record for this book is available from the National Library of Australia

ISBN 978 0 14 377799 1

Penguin Random House Australia uses papers that are natural and recyclable products, made from wood grown in sustainable forests. The logging and manufacture processes are expected to conform to the environmental regulations of the country of origin.

penguin.com.au

We at Penguin Random House Australia acknowledge that Aboriginal and Torres Strait Islander peoples are the Traditional Custodians and the first storytellers of the lands on which we live and work. We honour Aboriginal and Torres Strait Islander peoples' continuous connection to Country, waters, skies and communities. We celebrate Aboriginal and Torres Strait Islander stories, traditions and living cultures; and we pay our respects to Elders past and present.

This book belongs to

_____

I once had a beautiful garden that for a long time I missed very much, but I have come to believe that it isn't the garden itself I missed — it was the nature of the experiences I enjoyed there.

This book is a collection of ideas inspired by my time in that garden and the happiness it brought. The activities I have shared take you from the indoors to your forever-expanding outdoor world; they don't necessarily need a garden but rather a sense of adventure and a willingness to explore. The rewards will be endless!

The journey of putting these pages together has been a truly lovely — and long overdue — exercise in being present. Of pausing to really be in the moment. Of reflecting alone and also enjoying the company of the people I love. My monkey mind was forced to slow down for a change, to stroll through days rather than rush.

Creating this book also gifted me time with my seven-year-old daughter, Mae, and our very naughty but very adorable puppy, Annie (meet her on page 73). Observing what naturally lights the fire inside Mae jogged my childhood memory and served as a gentle nudge to re-create the joys of those days and appreciate the importance of play. For children and adults alike, play means we can do anything or be anyone regardless of who we are in our everyday lives. The beauty of seeing unencumbered, unselfconscious play and unlimited imagination has inspired me to move forward in a similar fashion whenever I can in this busy world.

To bring all of this together for you, we tested recipes, pulled out our pencils and paints to create self-portraits, threw together a summer dance party, headed out to explore our neighbourhood on our bikes and simply reflected on what fills our days and rewards our hearts. We plan to continue this love of everyday play, every day.

I wrote this book reflecting on nature, and the ideas are arranged by season. But you don't have to limit yourself to exploring them in any particular order. That's the thing about ideas — they're just ideas, sparks of inspiration, and it's up to you to action them. Turn to the index at the back to find the page number for the recipes and activities that can brighten your day.

My hope is that this book encourages joy in your home and in your heart. I want it to remind you that simple is best, your imagination is a gift and time with family and friends (whether that be getting busy at the beach, making mess in your kitchen or silently snuggling on the couch) is to be treasured.

kate

Autumn

There is something about autumn that keeps you guessing. The buzz of a festive season full of swimming and sunshine is over. March rolls in and brings with it a sense of things slowing down, growing calm, quietening, yet the streets and skylines are awash with loud, vibrant colour. Red, amber, orange and yellow fireworks explode in the autumnal air. Look around! It really is glorious.

The days grow cooler and the nights can feel cold. Is it time to dig out those knitted jumpers and thick socks? I look forward to long (less sweaty) weekend walks.

Autumn is the time to take a breath, to notice the gentle passing of time by watching the way our world changes around us. Take time to soak it in and acknowledge that as the seasons change, so do we and that's okay.

Everything about autumn feels golden. The gardens, the glow under my front door as I arrive home each evening. Even the air. Autumn is good. Autumn is a warm hug.

RASPBERRY JAM

When you look at all the excellent varieties of jam in your local grocery store or weekend farmers' market, it's easy to ask, 'Why would I make my own?' But what if I told you that this recipe for raspberry jam is super simple and super tasty — and you'll need just a little help from a grown-up?

Spread your jam on toast, add a large dollop to scones or let it be the star of your next culinary creation.

INGREDIENTS

2 cups mushed raspberries

2 cups caster sugar

2 teaspoons lemon juice

Sterilised jars

HOW DO I STERILISE JARS?

Try one of the following options.

- Submerge in boiling water for 10 minutes.
- Bake in the oven for 15 minutes at 180°C.
- Wash thoroughly in hot, soapy water.
- Run through a hot cycle in your dishwasher.

METHOD

1. Place your raspberries in a heavy-based saucepan over a medium heat. Bring to the boil and cook for 3 minutes — be careful not to burn the berries! — then remove from the heat.

2. Add the caster sugar and lemon juice, and stir well. Bring the mixture back to the boil, stirring constantly, and cook for another 3 minutes or until the sugar has dissolved and your mixture has thickened. Remove from the heat.

3. Pour the jam into your sterilised jars. Seal the lids immediately, and store in a cool place. When you have opened your jam, be sure to keep it in the fridge.

RASPBERRY AND COCONUT SLICE

Want to put your raspberry jam to work right away?

INGREDIENTS

½ cup icing sugar

1 cup plain flour

¾ cup desiccated coconut

115 grams butter, melted

¾ cup homemade raspberry jam (you'll find the recipe on page 3)

1 large egg

¼ cup caster sugar

½ teaspoon vanilla extract

1½ cups shredded coconut

METHOD

1. Preheat your oven to 180°C. Grease and line a 20-centimetre square tin with baking paper.

2. In a large bowl, combine the icing sugar, flour and desiccated coconut. Add the melted butter and stir until the mixture resembles wet sand.

3. Use the back of a spoon to press the mixture into your lined baking tin until it forms an even layer. Pop this in the oven and bake for 10–12 minutes or until the edges are slightly golden.

4. Remove from the oven and, while the base is still warm, spread evenly with jam.

5. In another mixing bowl, whisk together the egg, caster sugar and vanilla extract until well combined, then stir in the shredded coconut. Carefully spread this coconut meringue over the jam. It might look a bit rough and patchy, but that's okay!

6. Pop it back in the oven and bake for 12–15 minutes or until the top turns golden brown.

7. Remove from the oven and allow to cool completely in the pan, then cut into squares to serve.

Write a Story

Sometimes the coolest thing about reading a story is not knowing what's going to happen next. All the twists and unexpected turns are what make you excitedly read the next chapter . . . and the next . . . all the way to the end.

You can join creative forces with friends or family and write your own story that is just as exciting. Start by writing the first chapter, then give it to your writing partner to create Chapter Two. Pass the story back and forth, writing a chapter each, until you have a complete story filled with characters you love and adventures you would like to go on.

Relinquishing control of your storytelling and working together to create your adventure one chapter at a time might be a real creative challenge for you and could take your story in directions you never anticipated. Good luck!

MAKE A WORRY DOLL

A Worry Doll can help lighten your load. These tiny handcrafted dolls originated in South America, and legend has it they represent an ancient princess who received a special gift from the sun god that allowed her to solve any problem a human could worry about. That's a big job for one princess, but what a beautiful notion.

Why not make your own Worry Doll? You can pop it under your pillow and sleep soundly in the hope that the princess will solve your problems, protect and soothe you and even ward off bad dreams.

Do you have some pipe cleaners or wooden pegs? And some colourful wool or string? Let's get started!

Add dots for the eyes.

Tie a knot around the peg to hold the wool in place.

Wrap the wool tightly around the peg, ensuring you cover the knot.

Use glue to stick some wool to the head. Cut to create some funky hairstyles.

You can alternate colours to create fun patterns.

MAKE AN EASTER HAT

When it comes to creating an Easter hat, remember: the bigger, the brighter and the zanier the better! Nothing is off limits when it comes to designing a beautiful bonnet, a towering chocolate crown fit for a king or an oversized bunny with a bad attitude.

Think about the following as you plan your masterpiece.

- What will you use as your base? Sunhat? Baseball cap? Headband?

- Do you need to sketch your plan before getting to work?

- Don't be fussy! Raid the arts-and-crafts cupboard at home for anything and everything.

- How will you secure the creation to your head? Easter hats can get heavy!

- Will you need Easter eggs to decorate it? Or to snack on and get you in the Easter mood?

EASTER EGG HUNT

IMPORTANT Grown-ups like chocolate too, so to stop them stealing yours, why not plan an Easter egg hunt just for the adults in your house?

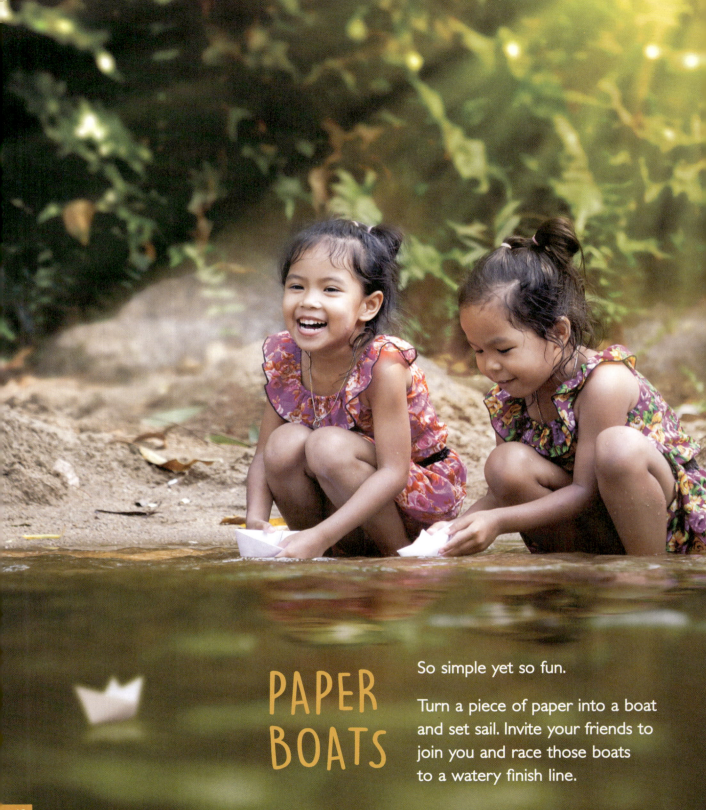

PAPER BOATS

So simple yet so fun.

Turn a piece of paper into a boat and set sail. Invite your friends to join you and race those boats to a watery finish line.

BUILD AN OUTDOOR FORT

Humans have been building forts for thousands of years, mostly for defence and protection the world over.

Today, though, you are going to construct a fort just for fun!

The great thing about creating a fort (and the story attached to it) is that you can use anything you like. Most importantly, your imagination.

Build it high, build it low. As long as you protect what's on the inside and **KEEP OUT!** what's on the outside.

Your time starts now!

GARDENING

Where is your favourite garden? It might be in your backyard. Or a pot plant on a balcony. Maybe it's the enormous botanic garden in your home city. Does it have an abundance of flora and fauna? Loads of birds and bugs and beautiful wildlife working together, calling it home?

Working in a garden takes patience but it will reward you with:

- A gentle adventure.

- Company and comfort.

- A sense of achievement.

- A secret escape.

- A silent and loyal friend.

The garden is my happy place. Where is yours?

SLEEP. REST. SLOW DOWN.

Sometimes it's hard to get to sleep. But your body and mind need — and deserve — to rest.

Did you know that while you sleep, your brain is still working? It's busy sorting and storing information from your day. It's also doing the important job of creating memories — and you don't want to miss out on keeping those!

Life can be very busy, so remember that rest and quiet time at home is important to help you feel and perform better during your days.

Try to do something relaxing for yourself every single day.

Snuggle on the couch.

Read a chapter of your book.

Thread beads.

Stare at the ceiling and maybe even snooze.

Talk to your pet.

Colour in.

Play with play dough (you can even make your own — see how on page 66).

PIZZA

Can every night be Pizza Night?

The answer is, no.

Can Friday night be Pizza Night?

The answer is, yes! Let's do it!

WHAT YOU NEED FOR YOUR PIZZA NIGHT

- Pizza!
- People you love to hang out with and who love to eat pizza.
- Drinks.
- Sleeping bags, blankets and pillows.
- A movie you all voted in.
- Popcorn to finish.
- And probably more drinks because pizza and popcorn can tend to be a little, or a lot, salty!

INGREDIENTS

1 Lebanese bread round or pre-made pizza base

⅓ cup passata

1 cup grated cheese

1 cup your chosen topping

TOPPING SUGGESTIONS

- Mushrooms
- Ham, tomato and basil
- Pepperoni and olives

METHOD

1. Preheat your fan-forced oven to 200°C.

2. Place your Lebanese bread or pizza base on a baking tray. Spread evenly with passata, making sure you don't quite spread to the edges.

3. Sprinkle most of the cheese over your base and then sprinkle over your topping of choice and finish with the remaining cheese.

4. Bake for 12–15 minutes or until the cheese has melted.

5. Enjoy! (And leave some room for popcorn.)

MAKE A BUSH PUPPET

Autumn brings an incredible display and array of colour on trees – pinks, purples, reds, yellows and browns. Have you ever stood still while a gust of wind blows leaves from their branches all around you? It's like being caught in an amber snowfall.

Those glorious colours and interesting shapes are a great starting point for getting creative. Have you ever made a bush puppet? It's easy! Head to the park or pick up the leaves that catch your eye on your way home from school. Spread them out. Divide them into shapes and shades and listen to what they tell you.

What do they want to become?

The warm glow of a sunset?

The colourful feathered display of a peacock's tail?

The burning embers of a comet?

The spikes of an echidna?

An autumn-inspired rainbow?

Fill in the blanks with your paper and pencils, and maybe a spot of glue, and let nature do the rest.

AWAKEN YOUR INNER SUPERHERO

Do you have a costume box to raid? Who might you become? A spy? A prima ballerina? A superhero? Get your friends involved and step into an exciting new world of adventure for the day.

PAINT A PEBBLE, REVAMP A ROCK

A tiny pebble in your trainer can ruin a lovely walk. But keep your eyes out for the pumped-up variety, because a pesky pebble can become anything: a ladybird, the slimy scales of a fish, a fairy house or even a good-luck charm with a special message for someone you love.

The pebble's cranky cousin, the rock, can also take on a new persona. With some paint, paintbrushes, marker pens and a steady hand, could you create a toad or some kind of extraterrestrial life form?

Pop some eyes on a rock, and it's the perfect pet. It never needs a run at the park and it won't mind if you forget to feed it!

START A BOOK CLUB

A book club can create wonderfully exciting discussions. You can delve into stories, scenes and characters you love, and those you really don't like.

Why not start a book club with your friends? You all choose a book, and for each one, you make your way through the pages at the same pace. It could be a chapter a week or the entire book, cover to cover, in just a few days. You might already own a copy, or perhaps borrow it from the library.

As the plot unfolds with all its twists and turns, you stop reading and meet to discuss it. You can do this during your lunch break at school, or maybe on the weekend via Zoom. It doesn't really matter where or when, as long as you can talk freely about all the things you love, don't love, feel unsure about, want to read again and everything in between.

What is important is that everyone is entitled to their opinion and their time with the talking stick! You can take turns to run the meeting or pose a question about what you have just read.

And remember – not everyone will like the characters you like or the choices they make. That's what makes book clubs – and storytelling – so much fun.

TRADE TALES

Why not start a regular book swap with your friends? Swapping books instantly increases your reading options and means you'll have people to talk about all your favourite book characters with.

REMEMBER

- It's okay to keep hold of your absolute favourite books that you think you'll read again. Or ask your friends to swap them back once they are done.

- Make sure you return any borrowed books in the condition they came to you.

- Never ruin the end of a good book before your friends finish reading.

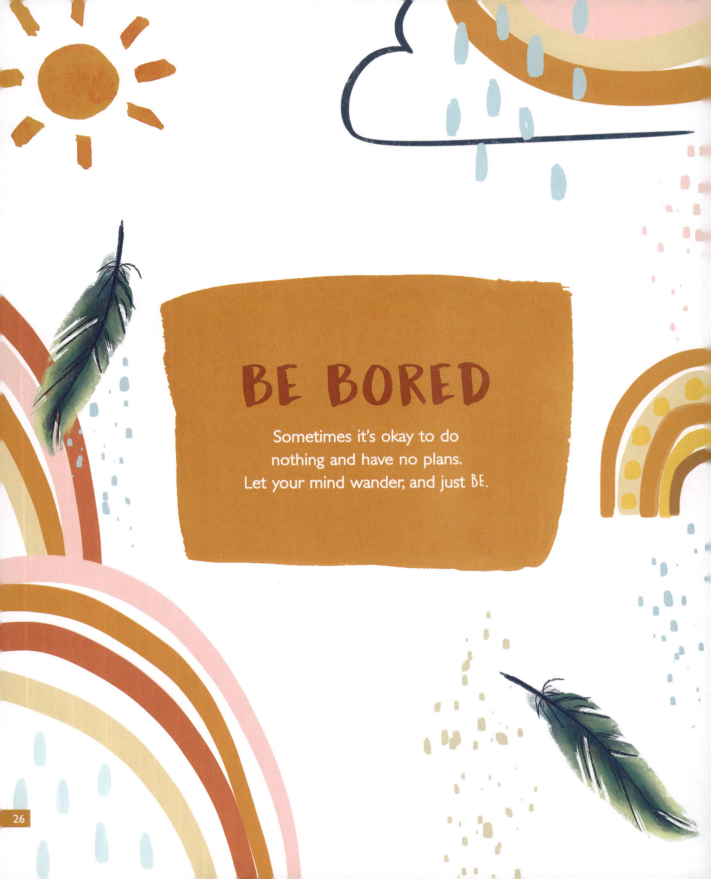

BE BORED

Sometimes it's okay to do nothing and have no plans. Let your mind wander, and just BE.

START A COLLECTION

Is it time to begin a new collection? Here are a few ideas to get you started.

- Feathers
- Stickers
- Stones
- Leaves of all different shapes, sizes and colours
- Jars and bottles
- Stationery
- Masks
- Ribbons
- Trading cards for your favourite team

MAKE A MOTHER'S DAY CARD

Every year, the second Sunday of May is a day to celebrate and remember the wonderful role mothers play in this world. It's a time to say thank you. To your mum or your nanna. To your friend's mum or even your aunty. To all the women who mother others.

There are many ways to make mums feel special, but I think the most precious way is to make them something from your heart. It's as simple as gathering your pencils, folding a sheet of paper in half and setting about designing your Mother's Day card.

Remember to write a heartfelt message inside. I promise, whoever the lucky recipient is will love it and most likely keep it for years to come.

MOTHER'S DAY BREAKFAST

These recipes are perfect for Mother's Day (or any other morning of the year).

INGREDIENTS

2 eggs

6 tablespoons pure cream (or full-cream milk)

Pinch of salt, plus extra to season

1 tablespoon butter

Pepper, to season

2 slices buttered toast

INGREDIENTS

1 ripe, sweet-smelling tomato

2 slices buttered toast

Olive oil

Salt and pepper, to season

PERFECTLY SCRAMBLED EGGS

METHOD

1. In a bowl, whisk together the eggs, cream and salt.

2. Heat a non-stick frying pan, then add your butter and let it melt. Pour in the egg mixture and let it sit for 20 seconds, without stirring. Then, use a wooden spoon to stir gently, lifting and folding your mixture over. Let your mixture sit for another 20 seconds then lift and fold again. Repeat this process until the eggs softly set while still being a little runny. Remove from the heat, season with salt and pepper and serve with buttered toast.

TIPS

- Don't let your melted butter brown – it will discolour the eggs.

- The less stirring, the better.

- Time your toast so you can serve your eggs hot!

TOMATO ON TOAST

METHOD

1. As the toast is browning just how Mum likes it, carefully slice your tomato into rounds 1 centimetre in thickness (you might need some help with this).

2. When the toast pops up, butter it and then place the tomato on top. Drizzle with a tiny bit of olive oil and season with salt and pepper. Yum!

Autumn is...
time to take a breath.

BIRD WATCHING

Think you have an eagle eye for bird watching?

Quiet time in your backyard, your local botanic garden or wandering the trail on a bushwalk can bring some wonderful surprises. As you wait and watch, you might see many common — and sometimes more curious — examples of birdlife. Each has its own uniform of feathers, its own traits and its own personality. It won't be long before you have your favourites who visit again and again.

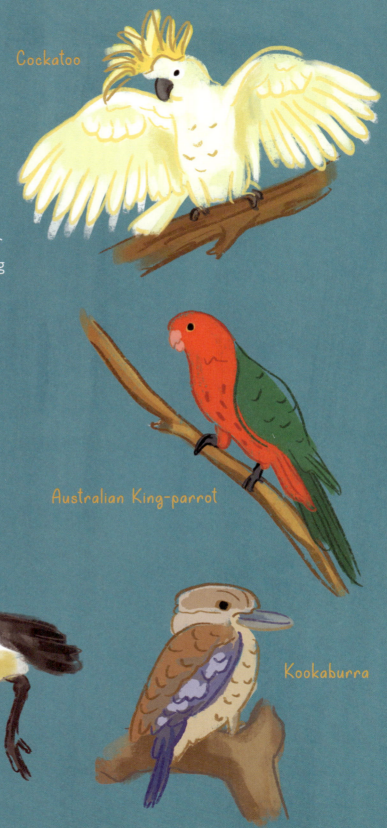

Cockatoo

Australian King-parrot

Ibis

Kookaburra

Rosella

BIRDS TO KEEP AN EYE OUT FOR

Australian King-parrot

Willie Wagtail

Red-browed finch

Kookaburra

Fairy-wren

Yellow-tailed black cockatoo

Spotted turtle dove

BIRDS YOU MIGHT SEE EVERY DAY

Magpie

Common myna

Noisy miner

Cockatoo

Seagull

Rosella

Pied Currawong

Ibis (Bin bird!)

Red-browed finch

Fairy-wren

PEANUT BUTTER BANANA SMOOTHIE

Makes 2

INGREDIENTS

2 large frozen bananas (always chop them up before freezing so they blend more easily)

4–5 tablespoons peanut butter (or any kind of nut butter you prefer)

1½ cups oat milk

⅓ cup quick oats, plus extra, chopped, to serve

Dash of maple syrup

Pinch of salt

JAR RECIPES

These recipes are excellent for breakfast but also make a tasty snack at any time of day. Make sure to sterilise your jars. (See page 3 for tips on how to do this.)

METHOD

1. Place all the ingredients in your blender and blend until smooth. Pour into your jars and sprinkle with extra oats. Enjoy!

MANGO AND CHIA JARS

Makes 3–4

INGREDIENTS

1 cup water

¼ cup white chia seeds

2 mangoes

2 tablespoons coconut yoghurt

Coconut milk, to serve

METHOD

1. In a small bowl, add the water and chia seeds and carefully stir together for 3 minutes, then set this mixture aside for 20 minutes. Over this time, stir a couple of times and watch the chia seeds become soft and creamy.

2. Meanwhile, blend the pulp of one mango until smooth. Chop the second mango into cubes.

3. Add ¾ cup of your chia mixture, as well as the yoghurt, to your mango puree, and mix gently until everything is combined.

4. Take your prepared jars and divide the mango-chia mixture between them. Top with your cubed mango and a dash of coconut milk (I like a lot!).

5. Keep in the fridge until you are ready to enjoy.

PATCH IT UP

Have you been lucky enough to travel? Or maybe you have a friend or relative who does? Collecting patches from all the places you visit can turn into a fun new piece of clothing. Or it might be patches from your favourite sports team. All you need is a denim jacket and someone to help you sew them all on.

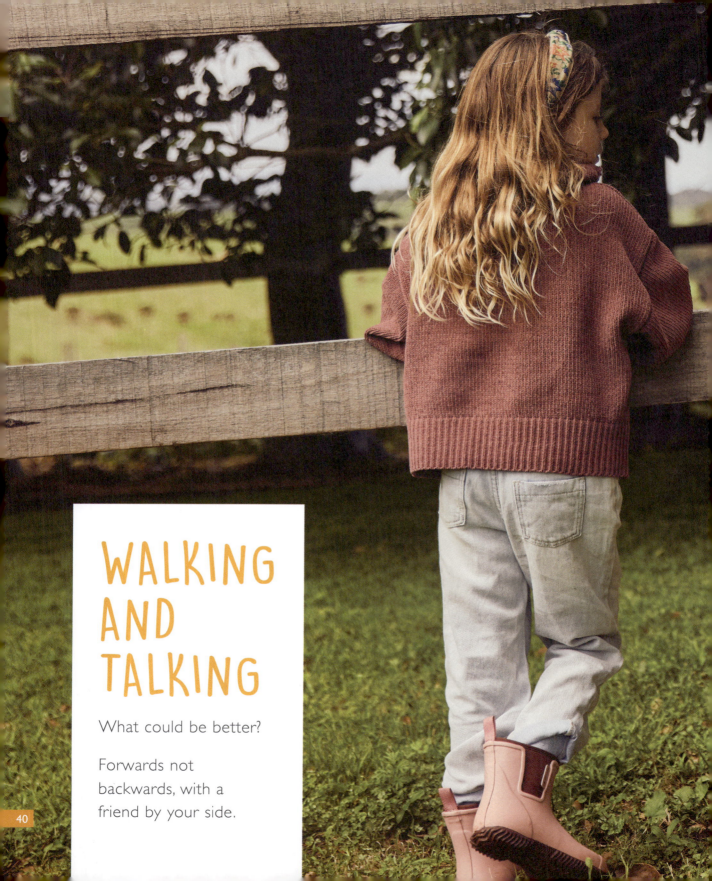

WALKING AND TALKING

What could be better?

Forwards not backwards, with a friend by your side.

Winter

For me, winter is the secret winner of the seasons. It's time to embrace the cold, to rest, restore and maybe even rediscover. But winter doesn't have to mean months of retreating inside. The cold can be where it's at!

Have you ever stood with your face to a wind so icy your cheeks burn? What about peering out the window on the first morning Jack Frost pays a visit? There's something magical in the *crunch, crunch, crunch* of the grass underfoot, and the *knock, knock, knock* of the frozen water in a birdbath that has transformed into a miniature ice rink overnight.

Inside, winter calls for daytime movies under the doona. It means an extra five minutes in bed in the morning. Warm drinks and warmer bubble baths. Flannelette pyjamas. Toast. Chocolate. Board games and chapter upon chapter before bed.

The wonderful times winter delivers are the ones that sneak up and surprise you. *Boo! I'm winter and I'm not who you thought I was!* These are usually determined by your attitude towards them. Am I getting wet socks or am I jumping in puddles? Laughing and learning. Only you can decide.

Don't let winter make you avoid the world. Instead, let it make you live in it. Soak up the wet and the messy and the 'my lips are purple' moments that make you feel alive. Winter is wonderful.

GAMES BONANZA

Devices down! It's time for an almighty games bonanza. Pull out every game you own that can't be plugged in, charged or turned on, and get ready for an afternoon on the lounge-room floor taking on your family and maybe some friends. The more the merrier!

If your home is overflowing with cheeky challengers, set up board-game stations. And remember to play fair — no cheating!

If the games cupboard is bare, don't forget the humble noughts-and-crosses, where all you need is a couple of pencils, a few sheets of paper and some strategy. Let the games begin!

MAKE A RUCKUS!

Do you have a sleeping baby in the house? No? Then this is the activity for you! Today you are going to become the drummer in your very own rock band.

It's amazing how many household items can be turned upside down to create a quick and coolest-of-cool drum kit. Buckets, saucepans, the dog bowl, even the washing basket. All you need to do then is borrow a few spoons and utensils from the kitchen and you'll be ready to bang out something that, if you're lucky, sounds like a tune!

** Make sure you put everything away once your impromptu concert is over, otherwise there will be nothing left to cook dinner with. **

THE MAGIC OF A WARM BATH

The sound of running water. The sight of bubbles. The smell of soap. The warming of your toes as you test the water.

A bath is a reward for your hard work during the day – all that learning and play and those thousands of steps you've taken. Now it's time to soak in the suds and wash it all away.

Lather your hair into a frothy crown. Slip beneath the watery surface and let your ears fill with water. Hear that? Me neither! Only muffled sounds of the heaving house around you. You may not even hear the call from down the hall, 'It's time to get out.'

Make the most of the magic of a warm bath. You earned it!

MAKE A SNOWMAN

Have you ever seen snow fall in your backyard? Or taken a trip to the snowfields? Either way, making a snowman can be a whole lot of fun, and there's no wrong or right way to do it. All you need is snow, a few fun accessories and a little imagination.

WINTER WALKING

Now is the time to take on the elements! It's so good to keep our bodies moving, even when the couch is calling and the weather gives us a good excuse to stay inside.

A winter walk is always an adventure. The air feels damp. Things around you look different, can you tell? You can actually see your breath in the air.

So, next time the wind is swirling or the rain is falling and someone shouts, 'Shut the door! It's freezing out there!', grab a coat and your favourite beanie and scarf, and tackle winter walking head on. Don't come home until you've jumped in the biggest puddle you can find. I dare you!

Street art by Jamie Preisz

LEARN TO KNIT

Speaking of grabbing your favourite beanie or scarf . . . A homemade scarf, hand-knitted with love, is my favourite kind.

Do you already have the almighty skill of knitting? Well done, you. If not, starting with a simple scarf is the best way to learn.

For tips and instructions, refer to your local knitting clubs, how-to-knit books, online video tutorials or one-on-one lessons with a family member.

HOT, HOT, HOT CHOCOLATE

Is there anything better on a winter day than coming in from the cold and being met with a mug of hot chocolate? I don't think so!

But hot chocolate is a very personal thing. How much chocolate is too much chocolate? Is there such a thing? Do you heat it first or let the milk do the melting? Stove top or microwave? To serve with marshmallows, or not to serve with marshmallows? Now, that is the question.

YUM!

THE ULTIMATE CHEESE TOASTIE

What goes better with a decadent hot chocolate than a gooey, oozy cheese toastie? Here are some ideas to make the perfect one.

Half cheddar + half mozzarella

Mustard

A cup of tomato soup to dip it into!

Pickles

A smear of Vegemite

Salt and pepper

White, wholemeal or multigrain bread

Ham or tomato, or both

Butter on the inside AND outside of the bread

Monterey Jack cheese

LETTERS OF LOVE AND THANKS

One of the first words we are taught to say is **TA**. Followed by **PLEASE** and **THANK YOU**. These days, now that you're older, you most likely rattle these off without even realising you are.

And we often find the time to say the words **I LOVE YOU**, too.

But how often do we write them down? How often do we really think about those words and why we say them to the special people in our lives?

Little letters of love and thanks can help us feel grateful and show our appreciation to others for a tiny act of kindness or all that they do, every day.

People who might love a letter from you

- Your friend
- Your mum or dad
- Your big/little brother/sister
- Your neighbour
- Your coach

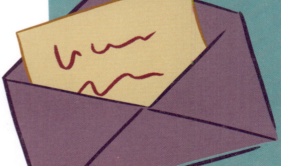

Your letters don't have to be long or complicated. They just have to come from your heart. You can choose special paper and delicately pen your words to leave secretly in the recipient's letterbox, or maybe you will scrawl your statement on a notepad and stick it to the fridge. Or you could send it via airmail as a paper plane! It doesn't really matter how you do it, only that you do.

HOW TO FOLD A PAPER PLANE

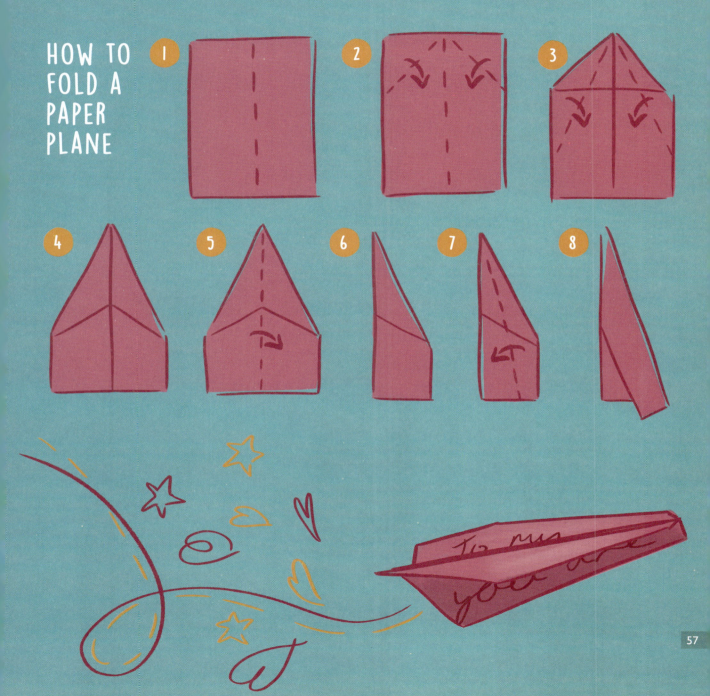

BUILD YOUR DREAM HOUSE

Let's go old-school for this one to create your dream home in your dream world.

YOU WILL NEED

- Old magazines and newspapers (maybe those flyers local real-estate agents drop in your letterbox)
- Scissors
- Sticky tape, a glue stick or a stapler

Flick through your magazines/newspapers/flyers for inspiration. Focus on the images of houses and the rooms in them. Bedrooms and kitchens, bathrooms and living spaces. Even the furniture that fills them. Pools and pets. Food and fast cars. Photographs of faces and entire families. Page after page. When you see something that catches your eye, tear it out and then cut it out!

Place all your cut-outs flat on a table. Assemble your world and stick it all together until your dream home in your dream world comes to life in front of you. And it doesn't cost a dollar.

STAR GAZING

Have you ever made a wish on a star and wondered what the galaxies beyond us might hold? Star gazing fills us with hope and makes us feel that anything might be possible.

The darker the sky, the bigger and brighter the light show above will be, which is why if you're in the country (or maybe even the desert) you'll see those twinkling stars more clearly.

Regardless of where you are, it's the idea of looking up, out of this world and into another, that is so intriguing. So, next time there is a clear, cloud-free night, rug up in your winter woollies, grab a patch of grass and maybe your sleeping bag and take some time to star gaze.

Orion

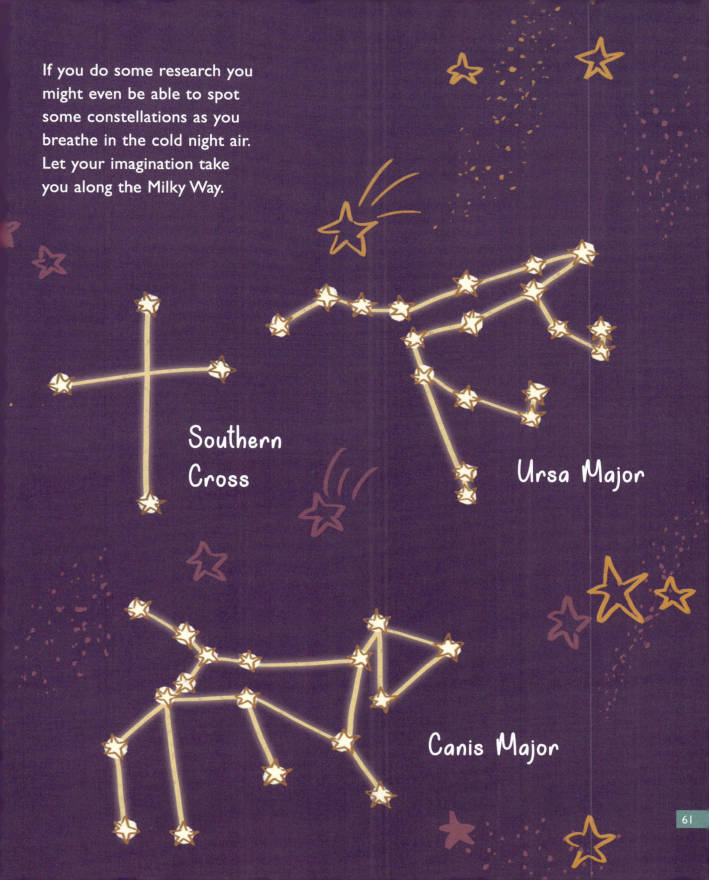

PAINT A PORTRAIT

Where to start?

First, choose your muse, your inspiration. Is it your teacher? Your entire family? Or maybe a portrait from a photograph of the grandmother you never got to meet?

Study your muse's face. Do you have a photograph you could use as a reference? Or it could be as easy as staring at your little brother at the dinner table one night.

Create a backstory for your portrait. Who is this person? Where do they live? What do they like to do? Have they taught you something important or done something you feel is great? What makes them stand out from the rest?

All that's left to do now is to put paintbrush to your chosen canvas. Your portrait might come together quickly or you might take your time. Paint a little, take a break, consider the mood and your subject again and then paint a little more.

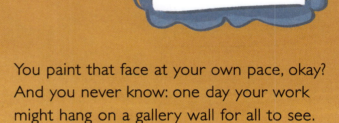

You paint that face at your own pace, okay? And you never know: one day your work might hang on a gallery wall for all to see.

THE YOUNG ARCHIE

Did you know that in Australia we have a portrait award called the Archibald Prize, which has been held for more than 100 years? Each year some of our most talented artists, young and old, are recognised for their incredible work. For even younger artists, like you, there is The Young Archie competition. Sounds like fun, right? Why don't you enter?

PANGRAMS

The quick brown fox jumps over the lazy dog.

So what? I hear you say. Well, the quick brown fox jumping over the lazy dog is much more than a disaster waiting to happen — it's a very special kind of sentence. It's called a **PANGRAM**, which means it contains every letter of the alphabet, from A through to Z, at least once.

THE QUICK BROWN FOX JUMPS OVER THE LAZY DOG is one of the most famous pangrams, but there are others. Set yourself the task of writing your own today. How tricky can it be?

INTERESTING FACTS

Pangrams are incredibly helpful to artists who design fonts because it means they can display every letter of the alphabet available in any particular design.

Pangrams were originally designed to test equipment such as typewriters. If you typed a sentence that contained every letter of the alphabet, you could instantly see which pad wasn't working. Now the same can be used to test computer keyboards.

PLAY DOUGH

No play dough? No worries! Use this quick and simple recipe and you'll be 'playing with dough' in no time!

INGREDIENTS

1 cup plain flour

1 cup water

2 teaspoons cream of tartar

⅓ cup salt

1 tablespoon vegetable oil

Food colouring of your choice

METHOD

1. Mix all your ingredients together in a medium saucepan, then cook over a low–medium heat, stirring continuously until the mixture has thickened and begins to gather around the spoon.

2. Remove the dough onto baking paper or a plate to cool.

Now you are ready to roll!

TIP

Homemade play dough is also a cool party favour idea. Fill small glass jars with an array of colours and push a toy dinosaur or figurine inside as a feature. Will you end up with the Ceratosaurus or the T-Rex? (Or insert your favourite dinosaurs here!)

PLAN A WINTER BEACH DAY

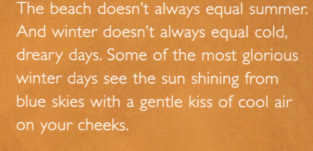

The beach doesn't always equal summer. And winter doesn't always equal cold, dreary days. Some of the most glorious winter days see the sun shining from blue skies with a gentle kiss of cool air on your cheeks.

Seasons and experiences can be interchangeable, which is why a winter beach day can be loads of fun. You might discover a whole new world out there on the sand, in the rockpools and — if you dare — in the water!

So, plan a winter trip to the beach. Will you leave your swimmers behind and swap them for your raincoat? Ha. Imagine that!

And if you're not in the water, try skimming rocks or sculpting a sandcastle. On wet days, the sand will be perfect for holding without having to run down to the water's edge.

HUMMINGBIRD CAKE

A hummingbird cake sounds delightful, doesn't it? And don't worry, I can assure you no hummingbirds are harmed in the making of it! It might just attract them, though, thanks to the sweet key ingredients of pineapple and banana. This nectar-like creation originated in Jamaica in the 1960s, and I have been baking it over and over for the past twenty years.

It can be made even more fabulous by baking two cakes and layering them. Thinly sliced mango makes the perfect filling, but all it really needs is its signature cream-cheese icing and a crown of coconut or miniature flowers. Or both!

INGREDIENTS

1 cup plain flour

½ cup self-raising flour

1 teaspoon ground cinnamon

½ teaspoon bicarb soda

¾ cup caster sugar

2 eggs

½ cup vegetable oil

1½ cups mashed ripe banana

¾ cup undrained crushed pineapple

250 grams cream cheese

1½ cups icing sugar, sifted

METHOD

1. Preheat your oven to 180°C. Grease and line a 20–23-centimetre round tin with baking paper.

2. In a large bowl, combine the flours, cinnamon, bicarb soda and caster sugar. Make a well in the centre.

3. In a separate bowl, whisk together the eggs and oil, and pour this into the well of dry ingredients. Add the banana and pineapple and mix to combine, then pour the mixture into your prepared tin.

4. Bake for 1 hour or until a skewer inserted into the centre of your cake comes out clean. Then, leave the cake in the tin for 10 minutes before carefully turning it out and cooling it on a wire rack.

5. When the cake has completely cooled, it's time to make your icing. Add the cream cheese and icing sugar to a bowl and beat with an electric mixer until the mixture is light and fluffy. Spread the icing over your cake, then decorate and serve.

PET PORTRAIT

You know that thing you did on page 62, when you set about creating a masterpiece? Now you are going to do it with your pet. That's if you have a pet, of course. If you don't, you could . . .

- Borrow someone else's. Be sure to ask them first!
- Find a photograph of a past pet and immortalise them.
- Draw or paint the kind of pet you would like to adopt.

Good luck getting them to sit still.

MAKE AN IMMUNITY NECKLACE

Want to make your own jewellery? Or perhaps an immunity necklace that can be passed around the family – whoever wears the necklace gets to pick a chore to avoid! Here's how.

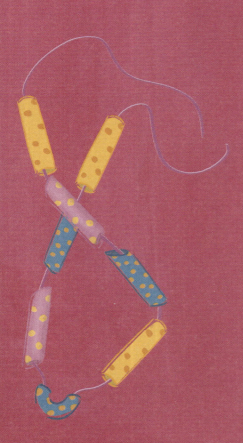

YOU WILL NEED

- Dried pasta (make sure it is tubular or easy to thread) UNCOOKED!
- Paint or permanent markers to decorate your pasta
- String, twine or ribbon
- Scissors
- Coloured beads, rings or cut straws.

INSTRUCTIONS

1. Start by decorating your pasta pieces. You might want to paint them different colours or use your permanent markers to draw tiny, intricate patterns all over them.

2. Measure out the length of your necklace and cut string to size. Remember to leave it a little longer than you'd like your necklace to be so that you have enough to tie the ends.

3. Get threading! In any order you like, thread your pasta and decorative items. You could thread the entire necklace as far as you can go, or make a simple pendant – whatever is more your style. When you're done, tie the ends together to secure your prize.

SPAGHETTI AND MEATBALLS IN TOMATO SAUCE

If you prefer to eat your pasta rather than wear it, how does meatballs and spaghetti for dinner sound? This dish is perfectly paired with some crusty garlic bread. A splash of olive oil and a sprinkle of salt always goes down well in our house.

INGREDIENTS

2 tablespoons olive oil

1 small brown onion, peeled and diced

3 cups passata

1 cup chicken stock

3 cloves garlic, crushed

1 bunch basil

¾ cup fresh breadcrumbs

2–3 tablespoons milk

500 grams beef or pork mince

1 tablespoon Dijon mustard

Salt and pepper, to season

Spaghetti (or your preferred pasta)

Your favourite grated cheese, to serve

Garlic bread, to serve (optional)

METHOD

1. Place a large, deep frying pan over a medium heat. Add the oil and onion and cook, stirring, until soft.

2. Add the passata, stock, ⅔ of the garlic and a handful of basil (retain the rest for later), and bring to the boil. Reduce the heat to a low simmer for 5 minutes and then remove from the heat. Set the pan aside while you make your meatballs.

3. Place your breadcrumbs in a bowl and cover with milk. Let this sink in until it's soggy, then use a wooden spoon to mix it all to combine. Add your mince, remaining garlic and mustard, and season with a big pinch of salt and a generous grind of pepper. Use your wooden spoon to mix it again until it is well combined.

4. Lay out a sheet of baking paper. Then, use a tablespoon to measure out your meatballs and roll into balls. Once rolled, place each meatball on the baking paper, and continue the process until all your mixture is gone.

5. Place your sauce back over a medium heat and warm it up until it reaches a simmer. Carefully place your meatballs into the sauce and simmer for 10–12 minutes – be sure to move them around gently with your wooden spoon so they don't stick to the pan – or until they are cooked through.

6. In the meantime, cook your pasta in a pot of salted boiling water. (Follow the instructions on your pasta packet, depending on your serving sizes.) Once cooked, top your pasta with meatballs and sauce, season with salt and pepper, then garnish with extra basil and sprinkle with cheese to serve.

PUZZLE IT OUT!

What's on your mind when you do a jigsaw puzzle? Nothing? That's perfect! A puzzle requires attention to detail: your attention to its detail. It means you can shut out the rest of the world. It's just you and the puzzle. It can lift your mood and improve your memory while teaching you skills such as problem solving and perseverance.

How about you make your own? For yourself, or for someone who needs a little quiet time. It's easy. You may not manage 500 pieces but how about starting with 9? You can work your way up from there.

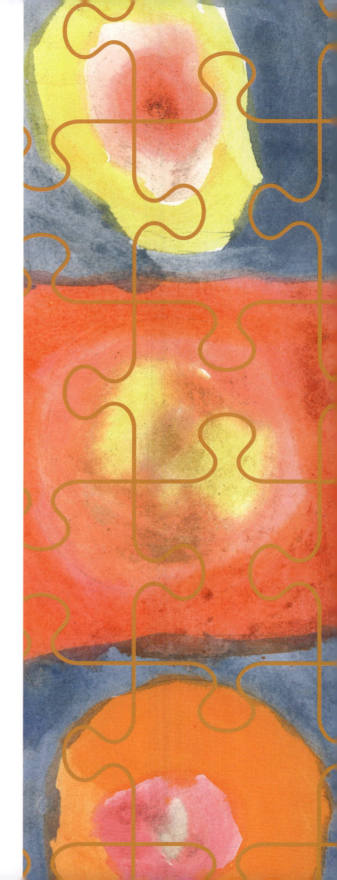

INSTRUCTIONS

1. Find an image. It could be a fun picture from an old calendar or birthday card, a printout from the internet or a favourite photograph that you are allowed to cut into. (If the paper is thin, you might want to glue it to a firm piece of cardboard that matches its size.)

2. Flip the image over and draw puzzle pieces on the back. You can use simple lines that make squares or something more intricate; whatever you like, as long as you can manoeuvre your scissors along them.

3. Cut along the lines. Slowly but surely your puzzle will fall into pieces. Can you see the picture you chose?

   There you have it. Your very own self-made puzzle.

NOTE

Why not give your puzzle as a gift? This will be extra special if it happens to be a photo of the two of you. Pop all the pieces in an envelope, addressed to your recipient. They will have to put it together to find out who their surprise delivery is from!

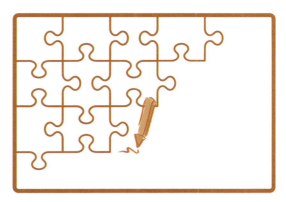

THE BEST-EVER CHOCOLATE BROWNIES

Now, I can't claim this recipe as my own, but I also can't give credit to whoever gifted it to me because I honestly cannot remember who scrawled it on a piece of paper and handed it to me many years ago. But thank you! And you'll be thanking them too when you bake a batch of these best-ever brownies. Serve them warm, cold or even with a scoop of ice cream. You're welcome!

Makes 24 squares of chewy, chocolatey goodness.

INGREDIENTS

85 grams butter

¾ cup caster sugar

¾ cup brown sugar

125 grams chocolate
(at least 50% cocoa mass)

1 tablespoon golden syrup

1 tablespoon molasses

1 teaspoon vanilla extract

2 eggs

1 cup plain flour

2 tablespoons cocoa
or cacao

1 teaspoon baking powder

Icing sugar, to serve

METHOD

1. Preheat your oven to 180°C. Grease and line a 20 x 30-centimetre tin with baking paper.

2. In a large saucepan over a low heat, melt together the butter, sugars, chocolate, golden syrup, molasses and vanilla extract until everything is combined and glossy. Remove from the heat and allow to cool for 10 minutes.

3. Whisk the eggs and add to the chocolate mixture. Then add the flour, cocoa and baking powder, and combine until smooth.

4. Pour the mixture evenly into your prepared tin and bake for 30 minutes. Turn off the oven and leave the brownies in the oven for another 10 minutes. Then, take the brownies out of the oven and allow to cool completely in the tin. Cooling your brownies in the fridge can make it easier to do this.

5. Cut your brownie into squares, sift over icing sugar and serve!

THE PERFECT SLEEPOVER

It's kind of funny that what we call a 'sleepover' sometimes doesn't involve very much sleep!

Do you remember your first ever sleepover? Did you spend it at your cousin's house? Or was it with a friend from school? Did you actually sleep, or just giggle for hours and keep everyone else in the house awake? Were there movies and popcorn or games and pizza? Was your room (or your tent!) full to the brim or was it just you and your bestie? Would you do it the same way next time?

When planning a sleepover, there are many things to consider. So, if you're about to plan another or take the big step of having your first one, here is a checklist to help make it THE BEST, MOST PERFECT SLEEPOVER EVER!

SLEEPOVER CHECKLIST

☐ Get your parents' permission!

☐ Invite your guests and give them a list of what to bring: PJs, pillow, toothbrush, etc.

☐ Set your menu. Will your guests arrive after dinner or before? Make sure you have plenty of snacks.

☐ Decide on the entertainment. How about a movie marathon? Is there a movie you have watched over and over but still want to watch again? Or something you have never seen? Ask your friends to submit requests before the sleepover. Remember to mix it up so everyone has fun. Oh, and promise to take turns with the remote!

☐ Make sure everyone is comfortable.

And lastly:

☐ Plan to have fun!

Spring

Spring always fills me with hope and anticipation. Winter draws to a close, the air grows warmer, the world around us begins to fill with colour and my heart feels full. There is something wonderful about seeing trees in my street show their first signs of the green leaves they lost months ago, and colourful buds appear in the garden. Something is about to begin. It's exciting. It feels happy. Spring makes me feel joy!

The beginning of spring also makes way for school holidays, which, if you ask me, is perfect. It's time to explore again, and we now have more time to do it.

SELF-PORTRAIT

The most important person in the world is you. You are precious and unique with lots of wonderful qualities. You are definitely worthy of your own self-portrait.

Where to start? The mirror!

When I look in the mirror, I see a woman with shoulder-length brown hair and green eyes with little lines creeping out from the corners when she smiles. She has pink glossy lips and a dark little freckle to the left of her bottom one. She loves polka dots and is wearing a navy sweater scattered in spots. She looks happy.

Now, you take a look in the mirror. What do you see? Who is that person staring back at you? Look closely, noticing all the special details.

Lay out a canvas (you might have a real canvas from an art shop, or you might use a big piece of paper), and take out your pencils and paints. All that's left to do is to put all the excellent things that make you YOU on paper.

Make sure you hang it somewhere special once you're done!

MAKE A COMIC

If you love drawing and telling stories, why not combine the two to create a cool comic? It could be just for yourself, or a gift for a friend.

1. To start, all you need is a clear storyline or a funny idea – and a willingness to have some fun. Think about how many parts there are to your story. Each part will need a step, and each step will need a box.

2. On a large piece of paper, use a black marker or pencil to draw lines to divide the paper into the right number of boxes. Each box is a step in your story.

3. Draw the star characters. Who are they? What are they doing in each scene/box?

4. Next, decide what they will say, and add the narration or their dialogue in colourful, quirky speech bubbles.

5. Watch your comic come to life!

ALIEN INVASION!

WORKOUT STATIONS!

Time to get your body moving, your heart pumping and your mind feeling fantastic!

You can do this backyard burn on your own or round up a group of friends and find a spot in your local park. Set up six different exercise stations and encourage each other along the way. Oh, and you'll need some music. Turned up loud!

Spend 1 minute at each station and then it's time to hit the next. Take a drink break and a little breather at the end of each round.

Here are some suggestions.

Star jumps.

Swing across the monkey bars.

Jog on the spot.

Do the plank!

Squats!

Can you do the splits?

Skip rope.

Find a step. Two feet up and two feet down. Repeat.

Can you balance like a flamingo on one foot for an entire minute? Can you reach down to hold your ankle? Try not to topple over!

Push-ups!

Walking lunges!

Parkour!

Punch the air. Fast.

Stretching.

SPRING CLEAN

Clutter can mean **CHAOS!** And as much as it's nice to have lots of things you love, it's also important for everything to have a home.

Spring is the perfect time to clean and declutter. Getting rid of stuff you don't need or use anymore can make way for the new, or give you more space for your special things.

Your trash might be someone else's treasure. Clothes, toys and books that have reached the end of their life with you might be ready to start a brand new one at another home. So, start by sorting into different piles. A pile headed for the bin or recycling. A pile to donate to a local charity shop and even a pile you could make a little pocket money from. There are plenty of online communities that buy preloved items.

I still have toys and trinkets from when I was much younger. Some are on display and some packed safely away in a box, which I look through from time to time. It's nice to think about the things you own that remind you of a special holiday, a special person or a special feeling. Always be sure to keep those. Just for now. Or forever.

MAKE A SPOOKY COSTUME

Is Halloween really about devilish disguises or loading your pockets full of lollies? You tell me.

Halloween costumes can be as elaborate or as simple as you fancy. Here are some spooky suggestions for you to celebrate the weird and wonderful world of Halloween in style. Be safe and stay scary!

Do you have a plain white T-shirt? Grab some markers or paints and create a scary scene!

Find an old sheet (check it's okay to use) and cut eye holes to turn yourself into a ghost.

SPOOKY FACE PAINT

Let your face be your canvas. Will you become a pilfering pirate or a scary skeleton, or maybe your favourite animal?

PIRATE

LADYBIRD

SKELETON

LOLLIPOP SPIDERS

So simple to make, these lollipop spiders double as a table decoration and the perfect party favour.

YOU WILL NEED

- Lollipops
- 2 pipe cleaners (approximately 30 centimetres) per lollipop
- Scissors
- Craft glue
- Googly eyes

INSTRUCTIONS

1. For each spider, you'll need 1 lollipop and 2 pipe cleaners. Cut both pipe cleaners in half so you now have 4 pipe cleaners.

2. On a flat surface, neatly line them up side by side and lay the lollipop on top of them in the centre. Now, wrap the pipe cleaners up and over the lollipop stick so that the lollipop is locked in place.

3. Bend the end of each pipe cleaner so they look like little feet. Place your spider the right way up and you will now see your 8 spider legs on the end of your spider body.

4. Glue your googly eyes to the spot where your pipe cleaners meet your lollipop stick.

5. Wait for the glue to dry, then scatter your spiders wherever you dare.

PUMPKIN LANTERN

Your local supermarket will likely sell pumpkins in the spring for this precise activity. They are softer to carve and easier to hollow than the usual varieties, but you will still need an adult to help you.

TIPS

I like to draw the evil eyes and the crooked mouth on the skin of the pumpkin with a permanent marker before I begin.

If you place a real candle in the pumpkin cavity to create a golden glow, be careful! And always blow out the flame when unattended.

Arrange jelly snakes to look as though they are slithering out from the hole in the top of the poor pumpkin head!

Journalling

Some days you'll probably want to write about what makes you happy, or excited or even giggly-nervous. And other days you might feel like sharing your secrets with your journal, to help you understand something that makes your tummy feel tingly or leaves you a bit sad. It could be a question you are finding tricky to ask or a feeling that feels . . . strange. But, that's the wonderful thing about a journal — it can be whatever you need it to be.

Writing things down can be a good way to express what we find hard to say out loud, and a place to share our good memories. When you start your journal, remember:

- It's your journal.
- They are your words.
- Begin when you're ready.
- And finish when you're done.

~~Looking after~~ Taking care of Archie was so much fun, but . . .

LET'S DANCE!

Do you like dancing? Then, like the old saying goes, DANCE LIKE NOBODY'S WATCHING! I mean it. Dance – really dance – like you don't have a care in the world.

Close your eyes (be careful not to bump into the furniture), turn the music up loud and dance to your favourite song. Go back to the beginning and do it all again.

Dancing is excellent exercise and makes you feel energised and free.

GO ON,
DO IT NOW!

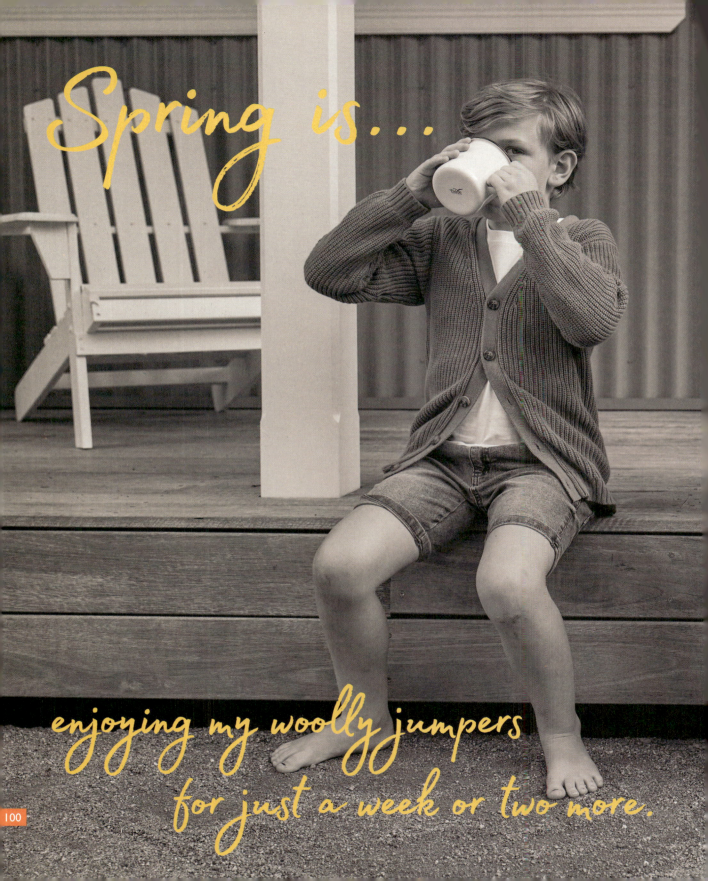

DEEP BREATHING

This special breathing will make your day brighter.

Find a big, beautiful tree with arm-like branches that reach up and out, stretching so far they seem to touch the sky. Or, if you're staying inside, sit or lie comfortably on the floor where no one will disturb you, and imagine you are under a tree just like that.

Think about all the green leaves high above your head. Thousands upon thousands of them, rustling together. Helping your tree to breathe too.

Now, close your eyes and simply breathe in and out. Notice your breath and the way it effortlessly flows in and out of your body.

In your mind, count your breath.

Breathe in 1 ... 2 ... 3 ... 4 ...

And breathe out 1 ... 2 ... 3 ... 4 ...

And again.

And now:

Breathe in 1 ... 2 ... 3 ... 4 ...

And gently hold your breath 1 ... 2 ... 3 ... 4 ...

And breathe out 1 ... 2 ... 3 ... 4 ...

And again. And again, relaxing into your breath, all the time thinking of your beautifully strong and sturdy tree breathing along with you. Sure and silent.

Ten minutes should pass. Breathing in ... and breathing out.

Slowly open your eyes.

Give yourself a hug and smile a happy smile.

SHORTBREAD

I love a recipe that includes just a few necessary ingredients but is packed with flavour, and this shortbread proves that more ingredients do not equal more deliciousness! Traditionally, shortbread signals a Christmas celebration, but you can make it all year round. There is nothing better than a piece of sweet, buttery shortbread with a warm drink, in front of a fire or on a sunny step in the yard.

INGREDIENTS

250 grams butter

⅔ cup caster sugar,
plus extra to dust

1 teaspoon vanilla extract

2 cups plain flour, plus
extra to dust

½ cup rice flour

EXTRA — JAM DROPS

If you don't have cookie cutters, or you love a bit of jam (or both), you can use this shortbread recipe to make Jam Drops. Once you've made your dough, use a spoon to divide the mixture and roll into balls. Place on your trays and push your thumb into each ball, making a well for you to fill with jam. My favourite is raspberry! See page 3 for a wonderful way to make your own.

METHOD

1. Preheat your oven to 160°C. Grease two oven trays and line with baking paper.

2. In a bowl, combine the butter, caster sugar and vanilla extract, and beat with an electric mixer until the mixture is light and fluffy.

3. In a separate bowl, sift together the flours. Make a well in the centre, then pour in your butter mixture.

4. With clean hands, shape the dough into a disc. Rub your rolling pin with flour and roll out the dough to your desired thickness.

5. With a cookie cutter, press out shapes and carefully transfer to your prepared trays.

6. You can enjoy your shortbread shapes plain, or decorate them. An easy way to do this is to pinch the edges to create a scalloped effect and prick the tops with a fork. Sprinkle with the remaining sugar, then pop them in the oven to bake for 20 minutes or until golden.

7. Cool your shortbread on the trays, and enjoy!

Explore Your City

It's easy to not really see things when you're looking at them every day. So, why not plan a day out to explore where you live? Whether it's a sleepy town or a big, bustling city, there are always things to discover and new experiences to enjoy.

If you never catch the bus, catch a bus. Check the air in your tyres and ride your bike. Or lace up your trainers and plan your route on foot.

It's good to ask a family friend or the smiling face over your side fence for suggestions. You can also google your local tourism website or visit an information centre to help with your planning – this is a fun option because you can ask as many questions as you like face to face, grab yourself a map while you're there and mark your places of interest like you're searching for treasure. And maybe that's what you will stumble upon. Little pots of gold in the very place you live.

Don't forget
- Comfy shoes
- A drink bottle
- A hat
- And a sense of adventure

MAKE SOMEONE'S DAY BRIGHTER

Isn't it lovely when you see someone smile? Isn't it even lovelier when you know you had something to do with it?

Think about the things that make you feel happy, that make your day brighter. Now, think about how you could do that for somebody else. And remember, a sure-fire way to make someone smile when you see them is to smile first. Try it — smiling is contagious!

Keep some ideas up your sleeve for when you know someone is having a not-so-great day, or just to show a friend that you really value them.

What makes my day brighter? Who might like this too?

AUNTY JILL'S SPONGE CAKE
with strawberries and cream

When I was growing up, my siblings and I would visit our Aunty Jill on her farm. I remember the distinct smell and the smoothness of the wheat as we played in the silos, and the excitement of collecting the day's eggs. The only thing standing between me and carefully filling my ice-cream container with their yolky goodness was the odd cranky turkey or two. Thankfully, Aunty Jill is not only a good cook but a brilliant bird wrangler! This classic sponge recipe — one of many I have stolen over the years — belongs to her and came to me on a handwritten note in the mail one day. It's light and fluffy and ever so pretty piled high with seasonal berries.

INGREDIENTS

4 eggs, separated

¾ cup sugar

1 cup self-raising flour, sifted

1 teaspoon butter

⅓ cup milk

1 cup pouring cream

2 heaped tablespoons icing sugar, plus extra to dust

1 cup fresh strawberries

METHOD

1. Preheat your oven to 180°C. Grease and line the bottom of a round tin with baking paper.

2. In a medium bowl, beat the egg whites until firm. Add the sugar and beat until the sugar has dissolved. Add the yolks and beat until smooth, then fold in the flour.

3. Heat the butter and milk in your microwave until the butter has melted and then add to your cake mixture and stir to combine. Pour the mixture into your prepared tin and bake for 20–25 minutes. To check the cake is ready, carefully insert a skewer – if it comes out clean, your cake is ready. Allow your cake to cool before removing from the tin.

4. To make the icing, beat the cream and icing sugar until desired consistency but be sure not to overbeat – you want the cream to look and taste light and fluffy!

5. Spread the icing evenly over your cooled cake, then decorate with strawberries and dust with icing sugar.

TAKE A TRIP TO THE NURSERY

Have you visited a nursery? It's one of my favourite things to do, and it might become your favourite too.

Wandering through the plants leads to some wonderful discoveries. You might spot a funny-looking plant you have never before laid your eyes on, or maybe you'll be treated to a fancy fragrance you couldn't have imagined. And: the colours!

The people who work in a nursery love the world of plants and are full of helpful information to assist in your first, or latest, gardening endeavour. So, if there's something you want to know, make sure to ask the experts. That's what they're there for!

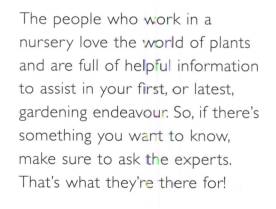

GROW SOMETHING FROM A SEED

Growing something from a seed requires:

- A seed
- Some soil
- Plenty of patience

I promise you, when you see that first glimpse of green poking through the dirt it will feel like one of your greatest achievements.

Growing a sunflower is a great way to start. The seeds are readily available and are easy to grow if you can find a sunny spot and some well-drained soil. (Usually you sow sunflower seeds in late spring, but I happen to think you'll be able to grow them any time as long as it's not too frosty where you live.) Here's what to do.

Use your finger to poke the seed about 3 centimetres into the soil. If you are planting multiple seeds, plant them 10 centimetres apart.

Water lightly each day until your seedling appears. This should take around 10 days.

Continue to water daily (not too much!) and watch your sunflower grow.

Some things to keep in mind about sunflowers

Sunflowers attract birds because of their yummy oil-filled seeds.

They take up to 12 weeks from sowing to becoming a fully grown flower.

They can grow up to 3 metres tall.

We can eat sunflowers seeds too.

If you manage to grow a few, they look beautiful in a vase on your kitchen table or are a sunny surprise for your neighbour wrapped in brown paper and tied with string.

They chase the sun!

Other interesting seeds to explore

Try growing an avocado tree. You'll need a seed, some skewers and a jar filled with water.

Bulbs. Hyacinths are absolutely worth the wait.

MAKE A FATHER'S DAY CARD

A FEW IDEAS

Fold a piece of paper in half and you're ready to go. Then . . .

Print up a photo and glue it on front and centre. (Don't glue the card together!)

Draw a picture of your dad or a fun activity you do together.

Even now I am all grown up, a big hug from my dad makes me feel like everything is okay. It's this kind of thing I like to say when I write in his Father's Day card each year, which he adds to all the cards he now receives from not only his kids (including me) but all the grandkids too.

A handmade card is the best! I guarantee, the recipient will cherish it. No pressure, of course! Just make it with love.

Include a funny poem.

Rose are red
Violets are blue
Dad you're the best
And I promise that's true!

Roses are red
And violets are blue
If I had to pick a dad
It would always be you x

DAD'S BREAKFAST-IN-BED PANCAKES

Pancakes? Still in your pyjamas? Yes, please!

INGREDIENTS

2 cups plain flour

3 tablespoons sugar

1½ teaspoons baking powder

1½ teaspoons bicarb soda

2 pinches salt

2½ cups buttermilk

2 large eggs, beaten

3 tablespoons melted butter

Cooking spray

1 ripe banana, sliced

Maple syrup, to serve

METHOD

1. In a large bowl, combine the flour, sugar, baking powder, bicarb soda and salt. Mix together using a whisk, then create a well in the centre.

2. Pour the buttermilk, eggs and butter into the centre of the well, then use your whisk to mix everything together. Try not to overmix – you don't want lumpy batter!

3. Heat a pan and grease with a light cooking spray (or a little more butter). Use a ¼-cup measuring cup to pour individual dollops of the batter into the pan. Let the batter cook until you see bubbles start to form. This is when you should flip them carefully with a spatula. Cook for another 1–2 minutes and then set aside on a plate until you have cooked all the pancakes you need.

4. Pile high and decorate with banana and then drizzle with maple syrup to serve.

LEMONADE

Freshly squeezed and shaken!

The best thing about this recipe for delicious homemade lemonade is that it doesn't involve boiling water, meaning you can pretty much do it all by yourself as long as you're ready for a bit of shaking!

INGREDIENTS

8–9 large lemons

2–2½ cups caster sugar (depending on how sweet you like your lemonade)

3 cups water

5 cups ice

TIP

Prepare your ice ahead of time. There is nothing worse than not having enough when you need it!

METHOD

1. Place all the lemons on your kitchen bench, then press down hard and roll them so they flatten a little. Cut the lemons in half and squeeze them (you will probably need to use a lemon juicer) until you have 2 cups of juice.

2. Find a large container with a lid. (Perhaps a big biscuit jar or plastic Tupperware container.) Add the caster sugar and then pour over the water. Close the lid and ensure it is sealed properly.

3. Shake your container until all the sugar is dissolved and the water looks clear. This can be hard work, so take turns with a friend!

4. Add the lemon juice, re-seal your container and shake again. That's it – you have lemonade!

5. Pour your lemonade into a jug filled with ice. The ice will gradually melt, so be sure to keep the jug refrigerated if you can.

LEMONADE STAND

Surely you can't drink all that delicious homemade lemonade on your own?

Is there somewhere safe outside you could set up your own lemonade stand? You could earn some pocket money, or raise money for your favourite charity. Watch the faces of your neighbourhood friends light up when they see you!

YOU WILL NEED

- A table
- A tablecloth for presentation and as many decorations as you like
- A sign listing your delicious product and the price
- A plastic container or purse for coins
- Your jug of icy cold lemonade and cups to serve (see page 123 for a delicious recipe)
- And, finally, a friend or sibling to share the fun!

Summer

Warm skin.

Swimmers with sandals.

Long, hot days.

The smell of a thunderstorm rolling in and the light show that follows.

The sound of lawn mowers and sprinklers.

School holidays.

These are only a few of the things that make summer hard to beat.

Maybe the arrival of summer stirs two completely different feelings in you. In some ways, it's the end of something, don't you think? The year is drawing to a close, with graduations and Christmas concerts. You might say goodbye to old friends and clear out classrooms. Even feel a little fatigued after all the wonderful things you achieved this year and all the challenges you faced head on. There is an imaginary finish line on the horizon.

On the other hand, it's the beginning of something new, too. So much to be excited about. Forgetting which day of the week it is because there are no school-day alarms or buses to catch. Is it Tuesday or Saturday? Does it matter? No homework! Just sleep-ins, bike rides and beach days. You might get yourself a part-time holiday job or be off to a camp. Christmas comes and goes and a new year dawns brimming with more of the same, safe, familiar experiences you love, but with the opportunity for the unexpected, too.

Lots to do and lots to learn. Let's go!

SUMMER BAY DINER MUFFINS

What better treat to pack on a summer picnic than some scrumptious muffins?

This recipe comes directly from the Bayside Diner and is thanks to a wonderful woman, dear old friend and cook, Carol Toohey. I enjoyed many of these muffins paired with a milkshake after a long day at Summer Bay High!

INGREDIENTS

2 cups self-raising flour

1 cup plain flour

1 cup brown sugar, firmly packed

2 eggs, lightly beaten

1½ cups milk

¾ cup oil (I usually use vegetable or sunflower)

MUFFIN TOPPING

¼ cup brown sugar

¼ cup plain flour

40 grams butter, chopped

METHOD

1. Preheat your oven to 180°C. Place 12 paper muffin cases in a 12-hole muffin pan.

2. Sift the flours into a bowl, then stir in the sugar.

3. In a separate bowl, combine the eggs, milk and oil, then add to the dry ingredients. Stir to combine, but take care not to overmix – the batter should be lumpy! (Said no-one ever!)

4. Add your chosen muffin variation (see opposite) to the batter, and mix to combine, then spoon the mixture into the muffin cases.

5. In a bowl, combine the topping ingredients, then sprinkle over the muffins.

6. Pop your muffin pan in the oven and bake for 20 minutes or until the muffins are brown and firm, then allow them to stand for 2 minutes before you remove them from the pan and cool on a wire rack.

MUFFIN VARIATIONS

Feel free to make up your own, too.

APPLE CINNAMON

2 teaspoons ground cinnamon

1½ cups finely chopped apple

Sift the cinnamon with the dry muffin ingredients, then stir in 1 cup of the chopped apple. After baking, sprinkle the muffins with the remaining apple and muffin topping.

BANANA WALNUT

1 cup mashed banana

1 cup chopped walnuts

Stir the banana and half the walnuts into the muffin mixture. After baking, sprinkle the muffins with the remaining walnuts and muffin topping.

FLOWER POWER

From a tiny posy on your bedside table to a messy arrangement in the dining room or even wound through your hair, fresh-cut flowers can brighten your day.

Maybe you have a garden of your own blooming with colour, or a neighbour who is happy to share. Have someone help you with the scissors and cut some fresh flowers for your home. You don't need a fancy vase. Recycle a jar, fill it with water and set about arranging your floral masterpiece.

And then you can draw one.

STILL LIFE

Still life artwork shows us human-made or natural objects. Sometimes these are arranged and displayed on a table. They never move, though. They are always very, very still. (Much easier than painting your pet portrait, that's for sure!)

Some inspiration:

- Cut flowers
- Fruit
- Vegetables
- Kitchen utensils
- Food
- Curious objects – clocks, coins, seashells

Lemons are a very popular subject for a still life. Is it their vibrant colour? Or the interesting shapes they make, whether solo and sliced down the centre or piled high in a fruit bowl? Who knows? But for today, let lemons be our subject.

All you need is a lemon (or two), a canvas and your creative tools of choice.

BEACH PLAY

You can't beat a day at the beach. Or a morning, a late afternoon or an hour, for that matter.

What are your favourite things to do when the surf conditions don't allow for play in the water? What can you discover on the shore? Make a day to do just that, but throw your swimmers in, just in case.

Collect shells.

Build a sandcastle, complete with a moat. Or a sculpture. You could set a timer for twenty minutes and see what everyone comes up with!

Explore the rockpools and the water's edge.

Dig so deep you hit water!

Pretend you're stranded on a deserted island and write an SOS in the sand.

SHELL ART

Shells. Tiny objects of art, all soft colours and swirls. Even the broken pieces with their worn edges are perfectly imperfect. They crunch under your feet and wash together to create vibrant borders where the ocean meets the shore. It's easy to spend hours fossicking in the sand, collecting handfuls of these sea treasures.

Use your collection of these beauties to piece together a work of art: a sandy mosaic or an underwater creature of the shelly kind.

Sign your name with a stick and leave your masterpiece for the evening beach walkers to stumble upon and admire. It's lovely to think that your shells will eventually be washed back into their salty home.

PITCH A TENT

Whether it's inside or outside, for sleeping or play, pitching a tent is the perfect way to get busy.

You might be a camping connoisseur with all the gear in your garage but if you're not, pitching a tent at home is super simple and easy to pack away once the fun is over. Rest a broomstick or mop handle over two chairs, then drape a large sheet or doona evenly over the top. And you're done!

What can you use your tent for?

Hide away and read in this quiet nook.

Gather your friends and tell ghost stories.

Fill with pillows for an excellent sleepover spot.

Use as your HQ for outdoor games.

WHEELS UP!

Wheels! Wheels! Wheels! What a clever invention. Some might say the most important invention ever. Think of all the wheels in your life. On your family car, or the pram you were pushed around in as a baby. How about your skateboard or your bike? And what do those wheels do for you? They help you travel, feel free and, most of all, have fun!

Take your favourite set of wheels out today. Fill your water bottle. Strap on your helmet and get cruising on a neighbourhood adventure direct from your front gate, or get your friends involved and plan a trip to a local bike track.

Nothing more, nothing less than the pumping of legs and the spinning of wheels. Set a record or take your time and soak up the sights. Try a new trick and feel the wind in your hair. I promise, you will feel awesome.

SUITCASE OF MEMORIES

A fun way to keep a special record of the year that was, is to create a paper suitcase. In this suitcase you can pack all your memories and unzip it to relive some of your experiences whenever you feel the urge.

Create this simple paper suitcase and then cut out the stencilled items and let every one represent a memory or experience. Pack your suitcase by gluing them all in one by one.

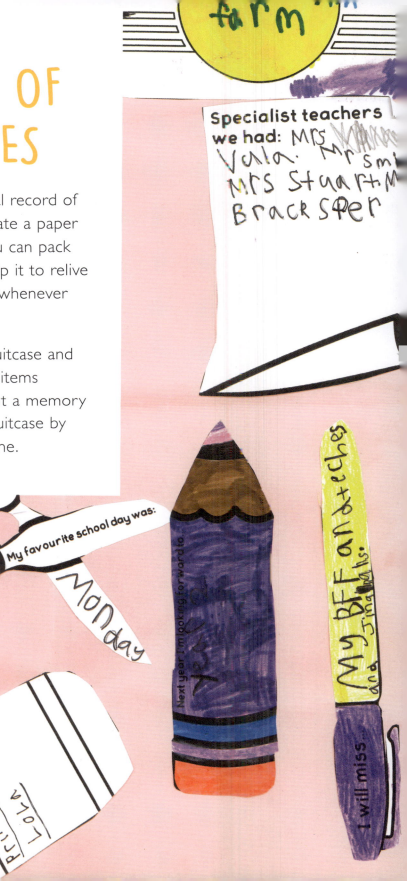

Here are some ideas and questions to get you started.

My favourite game to play was . . .

Something tricky this year was . . .

My favourite day at school was . . .

I will miss . . .

We went on an excursion to . . .

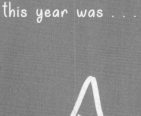

The coolest thing I learnt was . . .

Something really funny that happened was . . .

My favourite memory is . . .

Next year I am looking forward to . . .

LEARN THOSE MUSICAL LINES

Do you have an all-time favourite song that you sing over and over and over (maybe it drives your brother or sister CRAZY) and then, one day you discover that you have been getting the words wrong? I have. So many times. So many songs. For years.

It doesn't really matter whether you get the words right as long as you are filling your lungs and throwing your head back. But for today, let's say it does matter, because you are going to set yourself the task of learning your favourite song. Word perfect. Summer-holiday road trips are a perfect time to practise this, so pick your favourite song and play it in the car again and again and again.

Why not give your favourite pop star a run for their money and make up your own song? Then you'll never be accused of getting the lyrics wrong!

ALWAYS SAY YES TO SWIMMING

I guarantee you'll never regret it.

Swimming is something we can do all year round, but let's be honest — water always looks more inviting when the weather is warm and the sun is shining. So, thank you, summer, for the exhilarating experience of swimming. For the ducking and diving and plunging and all the pleasures of being wet. There are so many options: the beach, your local public pool, a nearby creek or river.

Swimming is one of my most favourite things to do!

I ♥ SWIMMING!

Some of the great things about getting in the water.

- It improves sleep.
- It's excellent exercise and works your entire body.
- It can boost your mood and help you manage stress.
- It's great for people with asthma and can help if you have an injury.
- Sea water is good for the soul!

Encourage all your friends and your grown-ups to jump in, too.

And remember: Don't swim alone, and always swim in safe, designated areas.

RAINBOW FRUIT PLATTER AND FRUITY ICE BLOCKS

The incredible colours and shapes of delicious fruits call out for a fruit platter as pretty as a rainbow. And then as an added summer bonus, why not make some fruity ice blocks, too?

Your local farmers' market will have an abundance of fruit ripe for eating and often a weird, wonderful and wide selection. So, choose whatever you like and remember to make it colourful! Blueberries, watermelon, strawberries and pineapple. Bananas, lychees and hot-pink dragon fruit. All full of healthy goodness and perfect to serve straight from the fridge on a hot summer afternoon.

A round platter is perfect for a fun display of juicy colour. Dice and splice your fruit with some help from a grown-up. If you have a melon scooper, you can create cute fruity balls of colour and arrange however you like.

For an icy version of this fruit goodness, you'll need a juicer/blender and some ice block moulds.

DISCOVER STREET ART

Warmer weather and longer days lend themselves to early evenings spent exploring your local area. On foot.

Many talented artists have splashed our cities in colour. Incredible murals as big as houses line walls, and words of wisdom adorn footpaths. Street art can be cute and creative and can also sometimes scream important messages for the communities in which we live.

For me, it's the boldness of the colours, the sharpness of the shapes and the amazing perspective that brings these artworks to life. Art in a gallery is beautiful, but art on our streets is truly alive.

149

Sundown Dance Party

Who doesn't love to dance? And who doesn't love a party?

It's time to unbottle all those fun summer vibes and combine the two with a super-cool sundown dance party!

You will need to decide your guest list, the start time and whether your dance party will have a theme or dress code, but most importantly, you'll need a dance space. One where you can swing those arms and kick those legs and not worry about knocking over furniture. Do you have a spare room you can transform or a lounge room you can clear (and relocate all the breakables)? If not, an outdoor dance floor can be awesome. Loop some fairy lights along the side fence and get your groove on while the sun goes down.

A barefoot boogie in the backyard is the best!

SUNDOWN DANCE PARTY CHECKLIST

◻ Your lucky guests!

◻ A dance space.

◻ A playlist. Make sure it's long enough to run the length of your party, and feel free to repeat some of your favourite tunes — sometimes once is not enough.

◻ Sustenance, because everyone needs energy to burn.

◻ A rest area for when your guests need a break.

** You can make sure everyone gets the chance to stomp along to their favourite song by inviting them to make a song request when they RSVP. **

SAUSAGE ROLLS

If you master this brilliantly basic and delicious homemade sausage roll recipe, you might never buy another one from a bakery or a kiosk. It was inspired by my friend Kevin, who made the most amazing ever sausage rolls ever for his granddaughter's birthday party. His version remains much better than mine for now but I am working on perfecting my own. You won't regret doing the same.

Makes approximately 30 bite-sized sausage rolls.

INGREDIENTS

4 slices white bread,
crusts removed

4 tablespoons milk

1 kilogram sausage mince
(store-bought thick
sausages are best)

1 onion, peeled and finely
chopped

1 tablespoon mixed herbs

2 eggs, lightly beaten,
plus 1 egg, extra, beaten

1 packet ready-rolled
puff pastry

Sesame or poppy seeds

Tomato sauce, to serve

TIP

Swap out sausage mince
for chicken if you prefer.

METHOD

1. Preheat your oven to 200°C. Line two oven trays
   with baking paper.

2. Place the bread in a bowl and pour over the milk,
   making sure all the bread is covered — you can
   break it into small pieces if you need to. Set this
   aside to soak for a few minutes while you make
   the rest of the filling.

3. In a large bowl, mix together the mince, onion,
   herbs and 2 of the eggs. Add the soaked bread
   and mix thoroughly — you might need to get your
   hands dirty!

4. Lay your first sheet of pastry on a clean surface,
   and carefully cut the square in half. Brush the
   edges lightly with the remaining beaten egg.

5. Arrange the filling in a long sausage shape along
   one edge of pastry. Then, roll it up!

6. Brush the log with the beaten egg and sprinkle
   with seeds. Cut into 4-centimetre pieces, then
   pop in the oven to bake for 20–25 minutes or
   until golden and flaky on top. (Then repeat the
   process from step 4 with your remaining pastry
   and filling.)

7. Serve warm with tomato sauce. Save any
   leftovers in the freezer for another day.

THE GIFT OF TIME

No doubt you love your family . . . and no doubt they love you.

Think about each member of your family and what your favourite things are to do together. It may not be a present you can wrap in paper and tie neatly with string, but spending quality time together is probably the best gift you could ever give them.

So, pick a day, pick the best way to spend it and invite your mum or dad, your brother or sister, or maybe your grandpa or cousin along. A day for just the two of you to do the things you love with the person you love too!

MAKE A GALENTINE'S CARD FOR YOUR BFF

Let's hear it for the girls!

We all love love, right? But love doesn't have to be the romantic, Disney princess, secret-admirer kind of love. Agree? So, this Valentine's Day let's twist the idea of saying **I LOVE YOU!**

Forget penning a poem to your Valentine or crossing your fingers for one in return. This year, 14 February is all about friendship, and you are going to make a **GALENTINE'S DAY** card and deliver it to your **BFF**.

Print a super-cute photo or draw a picture of the two of you and cut it into the shape of a heart. Then, tell them how special they are. How precious. What makes them such a wonderful, valued friend and how much you looooove having them by your side. You could list a couple of things you love doing with your Galentine and make a time to do them again soon.

CHRISTMAS TREE DECORATIONS

I don't know about your Christmas tree but ours is peppered with hand-crafted decorations, each year bringing a new addition of improved skill and creativity.

It's easy to make your own, which might take pride of place on your tree or that of someone you love. These ones are nice and flat, so you could pop one in the post to a special person who lives far away.

YOU WILL NEED

- 3 paddle pop sticks per tree decoration – you can buy coloured ones or paint the natural wooden kind
- A glue stick
- Coloured pipe cleaners or miniature tinsel threads
- A star for each decoration
- String

INSTRUCTIONS

1. Glue the sticks to make a triangle/shape of a pine tree.

2. Twist and thread the tinsel/pipe cleaners to create tree decorations.

3. Glue the star to the top of your triangle/tree and tie a loop of string to hang the decoration.

CREATE YOUR OWN WRAPPING PAPER

Homemade wrapping paper tied up with string. This truly is one of my favourite things.

Making your own wrapping paper means that when it's time to give your gift, every layer of it is straight from your heart.

There are two ways to go about this.

1. Buy a roll of brown paper and decorate it in measurements of 1 metre.

   For long lengths, painting is the way to go. Cut out a stencil on blank paper if you plan to use a paintbrush, or try stamping by cutting shapes in the hardest vegetable you can find. (Potatoes are perfect for this.)

2. Repurpose your existing artwork.

   If you don't have the materials or time to create your wrapping paper from scratch, you can always pull out some old artwork that you might like to wrap your gifts in. You most likely have an entire cupboard of wrapping sheets ready to go right now.

   Then, voilà! All you need to do now is enclose your gift, fasten with sticky tape and tie with string.

CHRISTMAS ROCKY ROAD

Some might like to call it reindeer poop (Okay! Okay! So it might have some visual similarities!) but I prefer to call it Christmas Rocky Road.

Creamy chocolate and festive lollies mix together in this very merry, delicious mess that can be broken up and gifted to all the sweet tooths in your life.

INGREDIENTS

- Chocolate (milk, dark or white)
- A selection of lollies in Christmas colours and shapes (think red and green jelly snakes or Santa-shaped jubes)
- Cranberries, pistachios or any other dried fruit or nut treat with a Christmas vibe

METHOD

It's so simple. Melt your chocolate in the microwave or in a mixing bowl resting over a saucepan of boiling water on the stove top. (You will need a grown-up to help you with this.) Then add your Christmas treats and mix to combine. Spread into a tin or dish lined with baking paper and refrigerate until set. Break into bite-size pieces. Box it up and enjoy!

NOTE

It's always best to sample your produce/final product just to be sure they are fit for gift giving/delicious enough.

MAKE CHRISTMAS CARDS (and gift with your Rocky Road)

Christmas is the time for giving . . . compliments!

Make your very own Christmas cards and fill them with warm wishes for a happy and safe festive season. For each lucky recipient, include a really cool compliment especially for them; one that you would like to hear yourself should someone think the same. Thank your friend, family member or school teacher for something kind they have done throughout the year. Tell them you noticed their act of kindness or all of their hard work. Share your favourite moment spent together and why it has a special place in your heart.

You might think they already know all this stuff. What if they don't? How lovely it would be for them to read it in your handwriting.

Deliver your handmade cards in the lead-up to 25 December accompanied by a little packet of reindeer poop Christmas Rocky Road tied up with tinsel.

ART POPS

If you can draw your friends and family, then you are well equipped to make these awesome art pops.

YOU WILL NEED

- Paper or card and coloured pencils
- Scissors
- Glue stick or sticky tape
- Paddle pop sticks

INSTRUCTIONS

1. Draw and colour your friends and family on paper or card. You can concentrate on their large round faces or include their bodies too – it's up to you.

2. Cut them out carefully.

3. With a glue stick or sticky tape, attach them to paddle pop sticks.

4. Give them as gifts or . . .

** Could be better than chocolate pops because they don't melt. **

** Could be worse than chocolate pops because you can't eat them. **

ART POP SHOW

Create an art pop ensemble cast and put on a funny show. Being able to control exactly what your family and friends say and do in your show will certainly be cause for a laugh! You could even add Santa and Mrs Claus and their elves, pine trees sparkling with tinsel, Christmas angels and the three wise men to make it feel truly summery.

To stage your puppet show, an upside-down shoebox with holes dotted along the centre makes a perfect dressing room. Can you add carols and your own festive narrative?

Maybe ask your brothers and sisters or your parents if they would like a starring role!

DISCOVER AN UNDERWATER WORLD

You might not be able to venture into space just yet, but I think exploring the ocean can feel like unearthing a whole other universe and therefore comes a pretty close second – for now.

Grab your goggles and get ready to discover what lies beneath the surface: a world that is wet and wonderful and, for the most part, welcoming. Dip your head below the waterline or, if you have a snorkelling kit on hand, be brave enough to dive below.

Learn some cool hand signals so you can communicate with your friends while you blow bubbles, and keep your eyes peeled for magical marine life. Maybe you have an underwater camera to record your adventure? If not, take snapshots in your mind and then, when you are back on dry land, create a colourful collage of drawings. You might even be inspired to research a cute creature you've never seen before.

** Always remember to be a spectator and not an intruder in a world where we really are guests. **

GOODBYE, WORRIES...

Warm air and cool grass.

Find a shady spot to rest and breathe your worries of the day away.

Lie flat on your back and place your hands on your tummy. Spend some quiet time with the most important person in the world and your very best friend: you.

Looking for something to do? Try these!

COOK

Aunty Jill's Sponge Cake 112

Christmas Rocky Road 160

Dad's Breakfast-in-Bed Pancakes 119

Hot, Hot, Hot Chocolate 52

Hummingbird Cake 70

Lemonade 122

Mango and Chia Jars 35

Peanut Butter Banana Smoothie 34

Perfectly Scrambled Eggs 29

Pizza 18

Rainbow Fruit Platter and Fruity Ice Blocks 146

Raspberry and Coconut Slice 4

Raspberry Jam 3

Sausage Rolls 152

Shortbread 104

Spaghetti and Meatballs in Tomato Sauce 76

Summer Bay Diner Muffins 128

The Best-Ever Chocolate Brownies 80

The Ultimate Cheese Toastie 53

Tomato on Toast 29

CREATE

Art Pop Show 165

Art Pops 164

Build Your Dream House 58

Flower Power 130

Letters of Love and Thanks 56

Puzzle It Out! 78

Self-Portrait 86

Shell Art 133

Still Life 131

Suitcase of Memories 40

Write a Story 8

KEEP BUSY

Discover Street Art 148

Games Bonanza 44

Learn Those Musical Lines 142

Learn to Knit 51

Lemonade Stand 124

Let's Dance! 99

Make a Ruckus! 45

Pangrams 64

Pitch a Tent 134

Spring Clean 92

Start a Book Club 24

Start a Collection 27

Sundown Dance Party 150

The Perfect Sleepover 82

Trade Tales 25

MAKE

Christmas Tree Decorations 156

Create Your Own Wrapping Paper 158

Fold a Paper Plane 57

Lollipop Spiders 95

Make a Bush Puppet 20

Make a Comic 88

Make a Father's Day Card 118

Make a Galentine's Card For Your BFF 155

Make a Mother's Day Card 28

Make a Spooky Costume 94

Make a Worry Doll 9

Make an Easter Hat 10

Make an Immunity Necklace 74

Make Christmas Cards 161

Paint a Pebble, Revamp a Rock 23

Paint a Portrait 62

Patch It Up 38

Pet Portrait 72

Play Dough 66

Pumpkin Lantern 96

Spooky Face Paint 94

OUTDOOR FUN

Always Say Yes to Swimming 144

Beach Play 132

Bird Watching 32

Build an Outdoor Fort 13

Discover an Underwater World 166

Easter Egg Hunt 11

Explore Your City 106

Gardening 16

Grow Something From a Seed 116

Make a Snowman 47

Paper Boats 12

Plan a Winter Beach Day 68

Star Gazing 60

Take A Trip to the Nursery 114

Walking and Talking 40

Wheels Up! 136

Winter Walking 50

Workout Stations 89

SLOW DOWN

Awaken Your Inner Superhero 22

Be Bored 26

Be Still 121

Deep Breathing 102

Journalling 98

Goodbye, Worries 167

Make Someone's Day Brighter 109

Sleep. Rest. Slow Down. 17

The Gift of Time 154

The Magic of a Warm Bath 46

Thank you

Everyday Play is completely and utterly inspired by my daughter, Mae, and therefore the biggest part of my thanks must land with her. Mae holds the most full, happy part of my heart. Always has. She is kind and creative, funny and clever and brings so much to the lives of so many. Thank you, my snuggle bunny, for all the work you also put into these pages. I would never have embarked on this book without you and no doubt you will inspire my next book and the one after that. Maybe one day you will even write your own.

Thank you to Leroy and Mia, Peter and Jack and Isla and dear little Molly. The nieces and nephews who contributed their personalities and artwork and who make being an aunty one of the best jobs ever. Thank you, Dad, for loving me and Mum for doing the same and thank you for the kilos of desiccated coconut you bought and the testing of your famous sultana slice (which didn't make the cut in the end!). Maybe next time. Thank you so much, Rebekah, and thank you, Suse and Uncle Blue. My memory of childhood is you. We did it together and for that, I am forever grateful. I know our fibro house with the white picket fence and the big lawn out the back in Chamberlain Street was our world and that shared experience can never be taken from us. It's who we are. It's where this book comes from. I love you.

Thank you to Mizpah and your beautiful family who have added so much warmth to my days. Thank you to Julie, Victoria, Bek and Bec. My dear friends, strong women and authentic mothers who openly shared their family journey with me before I ever had my own.

Thank you to Damian Bennett, who knew exactly what I wanted to deliver, I always knew you did, and to Erica Warren, who shared the incredible location that is Greyleigh. It sighed so beautifully and was the perfect energy for us.

Thank you, Erin Keneally. I wouldn't know where to start if I started listing what for.

Thank you, Claire de Medici and Zoe Bechara and all at PRH who knew I could create this wonderful reminder of childhood and encouraged me to share a lot of what I hold so tightly. You have allowed me the safe space to celebrate what is most dear to me. Your excitement and support has been unwavering and has reminded me how working on something truly connected to your core is the most rewarding of experiences.

And finally to Becca King. It is your illustrations that bring my words to life and will inspire the children who flick through these pages to find the extraordinary in every day. Thank you from the bottom of my heart.

kate